Contents

KU-376-303

Foreword   4

Note to teachers   5

What is worship?   6

Muslim worship   14

Christian worship   24

The way of the Buddha   34

Glossary and Index   47

Acknowledgements   48

Foreword

All people in all ages have searched for answers to questions about the mysteries of life and the world around us. How should I live my life? What happens when we die? Why was the world created? You too, I am sure, sometimes puzzle over these and other questions. There is never only one answer to such mysteries but the responses some people have made to them can help us as we search for our own. This book begins by asking you to look a little deeper at your own experience. It then shares with you some Christian ideas along with those from two or three other great world faiths.

It would take more than one lifetime to explore even part of the religious experience of mankind. The books in this series do not even attempt it. They simply take you into an important aspect of a faith in such a way that you may catch a little of the vision of life which lies behind it.

When you set out on the expedition through this book, keep your mind open to new ideas and you will find the journey fascinating.

The most successful travellers keep a record of their journey in order to build on their experience. In the following pages you will find suggestions for ways in which you can continue to explore and record your experiences in your own *Book of Worship*.

David Naylor
County Adviser for Religious
Education in Hampshire

Camdean School

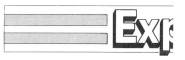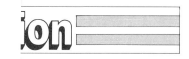

Item no.   00755

Worship

Olivia Bennett

Series Consultant: David Naylor
County Adviser for Religious Education
in Hampshire

Bell & Hyman
London

First published in 1984 by
BELL & HYMAN LIMITED
Denmark House
37–39 Queen Elizabeth Street
London SE1 2QB

© Olivia Bennett 1984

All rights reserved. No part of this publication may
be reproduced, stored in a retrieval system, or
transmitted, in any form or by any means,
electronic, mechanical, photocopying, recording or
otherwise, without the prior permission of Bell &
Hyman Limited.

British Library Cataloguing in Publication Data
Bennett, Olivia
    Worship.—(Exploring religion)
    1. Worship
    I. Title   II. Series
    291.4'3   BL550

ISBN 0 7135 2328 X

Printed in Great Britain

Designed by Geoffrey Wadsley

Note to teachers

The starting point in each of the themes explored in this series is the children's own experiences and feelings. These experiences and feelings are then related to aspects of the Christian and other religious traditions in which they find a parallel. The text aims not merely to give information but to stimulate the imagination of the readers, to encourage them to 'stand in the shoes' of the believer and so get closer to understanding the meaning which that particular religious act or concept may have for the believer.

It is not the purpose of the series to provide an exhaustive study of the world's major religions. There are already many books written for children which do examine each religion in considerable detail. **Exploring Religion** aims to complement such books by adopting a thematic approach in a way which encourages a spirit of enquiry, compassion, understanding and respect for both the similarities and differences between the world's major religions. It also aims to explore and show the religious dimension to life as being part of people's overall pattern of living, not a thing apart, and so there is continuing reference to the child's own experience. There is no assumption that any reader has a formal religious background or belief.

Activities

On many pages, you will find 'boxes' containing suggestions and guidelines for relevant activities, drawing upon and sometimes expanding the ideas explored in the surrounding text and pictures. The activities aim to foster the same spirit of enquiry and exploration into the meaning of people's religious experience. They, too, encourage the children to reflect and draw upon their own experiences, from the secular and everyday to, if appropriate, the more explicitly religious. They, too, should make demands on the children's imagination.

While most activities draw upon the material contained in the chapter where they appear, some may be more beneficially embarked upon before the chapter is read in order to prepare the ground for the concepts contained within it. Activities may be done by individuals, in small groups or by the whole class. Some activities are clearly one-offs, quickly accomplished; others have enough scope to take up much more time. There is usually some flexibility, allowing the teacher to shape the activity according to his or her needs and requirements.

Each title (with the probable exception of **People**) can be used to encourage the pupils to make their own book of **Festivals**, **Buildings** and so on (for example, *My Own Book of Festivals*). The majority of activities provide material which can go into these books.

Where children are asked to find out more about a particular religious ceremony or place, it may help to bring in a member of the community concerned, perhaps a parent or local religious leader. However, since the aim of this is to increase the children's insight into, and imaginative understanding of, that particular religious tradition, such 'speakers' must be good at communicating; mere weight of knowledge is less important. Children in the class, where appropriate, could be encouraged to describe their own experience of a particular religious act or place and what it means to them, although some may be too shy or understandably reluctant to do this. In both these cases, personal interpretation and experience of certain customs and practices may differ slightly, since followers of any particular religion rarely practise their beliefs in exactly the same ways.

Visits to religious buildings are also suggested. This may well not always be possible but full use of local resources, such as teacher centres, should provide helpful material such as filmstrips and artifacts. Where there is an activity along the lines of acting out a religious custom, care has been taken not to suggest anything which might cause offence to a member of the religion concerned. However, sensitivities will vary, as will the religious and ethnic composition of the classroom and local community, and careful judgement and discretion will be vital.

Care has been taken with the language level but some words may be unfamiliar and there is a glossary, and index, on pages 47 and 48. Biblical references are taken from *The Good News Bible* where the language seemed most suitable for the age range.

The children who read these books live in a multi-cultural society and an interdependent world, and the series as a whole explores many aspects of the major world faiths. It is recognised, however, that for most children in Britain any immediate religious reference point is likely to be Christianity and this plays an important part in each book.

Teacher's Guide

Accompanying the series is a 32 page Teacher's Guide. This expands upon some of the activities in the pupil books and contains ideas for more detailed or complex ones. It also provides suggestions and examples of ways in which activities can be built into topic work, and highlights the range of learning experiences into which the text and the activities can usefully be incorporated.

What is worship?

Make a list of the things in your life which are precious to you. Use the following headings:

People   Places
Things   Experiences

In a few sentences try to explain what is important about each one.

Do you know what the word 'worship' means? It comes from two much older words – worth ship. It means to think that someone or something is of great worth and value. Perhaps someone has used the expression 'hero-worship' to describe the way you or some friends feel about someone. Most people have been devoted fans of a singer, sports star or actor at some time. Many will have hero-worshipped an older brother, sister, teacher or friend for a while too.

Maybe words such as 'admire' or 'adore' are better words to describe their feelings. Often they wish they had the same talent, looks or way of life as the person or group they admire. They might copy the way they dress or wear their hair. They might try to sing, act or play sport in the same style. Fans of pop or sport stars often collect all the pictures and articles about them that they can find. They try

▶ Bob Geldorf of The Boomtown Rats. Most people hero-worship singers, actors or sports stars at some time in their life.

6

to see them play whenever possible. If somebody admires a teacher or an older friend they may try to do things especially well for them, so that their efforts are noticed and appreciated. But it is often difficult to express what we really feel in these situations. Sometimes we find ourselves behaving in a silly way when we are with

Imagine you were going to leave your home and emigrate to another country with your family. Who would you want to see and talk with before you leave? Who would you like to get letters from often? Why? Are these the same people you first thought of as people you 'worshipped'?

somone we admire a lot and then feel cross with ourselves afterwards!

If you think of someone as a hero or heroine, what is it about them which is important to you? Perhaps they have some quality or skill which you would like to have. Maybe you feel that they would never be worried by the sort of things which puzzle or disturb you. You think that they must somehow know most of the answers to all the things about life which you find so hard to understand.

The sort of 'hero-worship' people feel for film stars or sports personalities may last a long time but often gets forgotten as other things become more important in their lives. There may be someone, or several people, whom you once thought were wonderful but have forgotten about now, because they don't seem so important anymore. But anybody or anything which really is worth our devotion usually never stops being important to us, even if there are moments when we forget or don't recognise their worth.

Body and soul

Perhaps you have a younger brother or sister or friend who follows you around, copying everything you do. You may find this quite irritating at times! But what they are really trying to say is that they admire you. They want to be like you because they think you are marvellous!

Does anyone feel like this about you? Do you ever wonder whether the person they see and admire so much is the same person that you think you are? Sometimes the way we see ourselves is quite different to the picture other people have of us.

Imagine you had written out a description of yourself so that someone who had never seen you before could pick you out in a crowd. It would give them a good idea of what you looked like on the outside but it wouldn't tell them much about you as a person. Because there is much more to you than what you look like. There are all the thoughts and feelings and emotions which go on inside you. Perhaps it would help us to find out what goes on inside you if we took an X-ray. Do you think it would show us what is important to you and what makes you happy or sad?

But the X-ray of the man opposite doesn't tell you much about the person he is, does it? It doesn't help you to know what he feels or believes in. It shows you his shape and his bones but it can't show you the feelings inside him. This is because we are more than a collection of skin, bones, muscles, fat and hair. There is an important bit inside us which we can't photograph

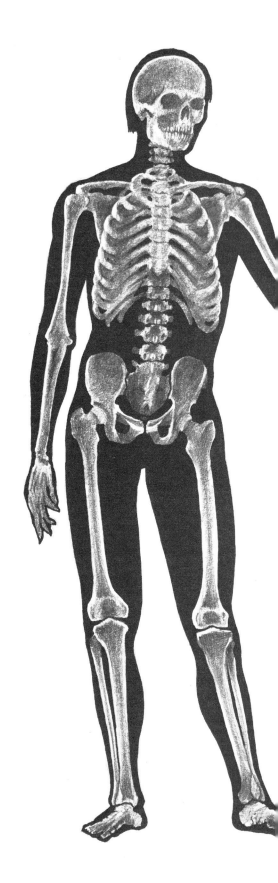

or draw or X-ray. It isn't even very easy to describe. Some people call this important but invisible part of us our 'soul' or 'spirit'. When people talk about the spirit and spiritual things, they usually mean something outside the ordinary everyday world.

Of course, our bodies need ordinary everyday things like food, water and shelter to survive. But this other part of us, our soul, isn't only content with ordinary things. It makes us want to find reasons for why certain things happen. It makes us want to understand why people suffer unhappiness. It makes us look for a meaning to life. Many people think that it is our souls or spirits which make us want to explore life's mysteries and seek answers to some of them.

Draw a picture of yourself. Make it the sort of picture a stranger could use to recognise you for the first time. Show the colour of your hair and eyes.

Would this picture tell anyone much about what you are like inside? Next to the picture, make a short list of what you are like as a person. Here are some of the qualities you might have: noisy, quiet, hard-working, lazy, friendly, shy.

Get together with your friends and look at each others' lists. Do they agree with your list about yourself or would they give you different qualities?

The mysteries of life

There are so many things about life which seem mysterious and difficult to understand. Even the ordinary world which you can see, touch and feel can seem full of strange and powerful forces. Just look out of the nearest window, for example. Even a dry crumpled leaf on the pavement has a fascinating life of its own. If you hold the leaf up to the light, you'll see that it has a delicate and complicated network of veins to feed it. Leaves unfurl and grow in the spring. In the autumn they change colour from green to deep reds, browns and oranges. As winter comes they fall from the tree, leaving its branches quite bare. What makes them follow this pattern? Why are there seasons in the year?

The mysteries of nature and life on earth have always puzzled people. And ever since the world began, people have created stories and legends to explain these mysteries. The Greek legend about Persephone was one explanation of the seasons.

Persephone was the daughter of Demeter, the goddess of nature. She was captured by Hades, god of the underworld, who wanted her to be his wife. When Demeter found out where her daughter was, she demanded her release but Hades refused. Meanwhile Persephone herself had taken pity on Hades and wanted to take care of him. Eventually a solution was worked out. Persephone spent half of each year with Hades and half with her mother. The Greeks believed that during spring and summer, when Persephone was with her mother, the earth blossomed

▲ The story of Persephone was the ancient Greeks' explanation of why the year is divided into four seasons.

▲ There are many things about the world we live in which can seem puzzling and mysterious. People have been asking questions about the mysteries of life for thousands of years – and many have found belief in a power, spirit or God has provided some of the answers.

with flowers, fruit and leaves on the trees. But when she left to join Hades in the underworld, autumn and winter came. The plants stopped growing and the earth went into hibernation, waiting for her return in the spring.

People have always asked questions about the world they live in. Spend some time talking with your friends about the things which you find puzzling in life. Then make lists of these questions and compare each others' to see if you share the same ideas.

The questions we ask

The changing seasons are just one of many things about the fascinating world we live in which can both puzzle and delight us. As you grow up, you will find answers to many of your questions about how things happen. People's knowledge about how the world works is growing all the time. But many of your questions 'why' may remain unanswered. Why must people suffer? What happens when we die? Why is there so much pain and sorrow in the world? Why are we here on earth?

You may explore several different ways of answering these difficult questions. You certainly won't be the first or the last person to seek the answers. As far back in time as we can tell, people have found some explanation of the mysteries of life in religion. Belief in a power, spirit or God greater than themselves has helped men and women make sense of the mysteries surrounding their lives and the world. All the ancient civilisations that we know about seem to have had some sort of religious faith. Religious worship is the way people reach out and communicate with the spiritual world.

11

Religious worship

We found it was quite difficult to describe exactly what the 'soul' was. It can also be difficult to describe and express religious feelings, which are very deep and important to people. One way of thinking about worship is to see it as the language people use to express these feelings. It is more than just words. People can show what they believe and feel about God by performing certain acts of worship. They pray, sing sacred songs, give presents and offerings to God, visit holy places and read holy books which contain the message and teachings of God. They have festivals and join together for worship in places built to show their love of God.

People use these outer actions, which are sometimes called ritual, as a way of showing their inner feelings. Whether it is singing a hymn, reciting a prayer or presenting an offering, religious ritual helps people to say what they feel and believe about the spiritual world.

The language of worship

As we explore some different forms of religious worship, you'll discover that people use music, art, mime, movement, words, paintings, statues, special clothing, and other things as part of the language of worship. Sometimes people worship together and gain strength and comfort from showing that they share the same beliefs. Sometimes worship is a very private act for which people prefer to be alone. So there are many different kinds of religious worship. Perhaps the one thing they all have in common is that the worshipper is thinking about something outside his or her ordinary world.

One kind of religious worship is to show devotion to God by travelling to a certain holy place. This is called a pilgrimage. Even a hundred years ago, going on a pilgrimage often meant a long, difficult and even dangerous journey. It was, however, a popular form of worship. Canterbury, Rome, Delphi, Jerusalem, Makkah and Benares are just some of the world's holy cities which have attracted millions of pilgrims.

Have you ever travelled around the country to hear your favourite pop group play? Do you think that could be called a kind of pilgrimage? Maybe you have followed your favourite football team to an away match. Football fans often wear special scarves, badges or hats to show which team they support. Sometimes they sing a special team song. Making the journey and sharing the experience with other supporters is part of the fun. Sitting at home and watching the match on TV is not the same at all! By taking the time and trouble to travel to the match, the fans show how much they support the team and care about its succcess.

People who make a religious pilgrimage also do so to show how much they care about God. In the religion of Islam, going on pilgrimage to the city of Makkah is as important as prayer or belief in God. In the next chapter we'll explore the meaning and purpose of this journey further.

Many football fans show their devotion to the team they support by travelling to watch every match they play. In this sense, the journey is a kind of pilgrimage.

Muslim worship

As far back in history as we can tell, most of the world's religions have had their places of pilgrimage. The object of a pilgrimage is usually to visit and worship in a sacred place or building. Sometimes it is to visit and worship with an especially holy person. In both cases pilgrims believe that their journey to the sacred place or person will bring them closer to God.

People of many different faiths make pilgrimages today. India has many famous centres of pilgrimage for Hindus, for whom this is a popular form of worship. Some of the world's centres of pilgrimage are sacred for people of more than one faith. Jerusalem, for example, is a holy city

▲ Pilgrims always visit the holy shrine called the Ka'aba. Muslims all over the world turn in the direction of the Ka'aba when they say their daily prayers.

▼ Every year, millions of Muslims make the pilgrimage to their holy city of Makkah, in Saudi Arabia.

for Jews, Christians and Muslims.

Pilgrimage is not a religious duty for Jews or Christians but every Muslim who has 'the health and the wealth' to make the journey to their holy city of Makkah should do so at least once in a lifetime. A man or woman who completes the pilgrimage may then add the title 'Hajji' or 'Hajjin' to his or her name. The word for the pilgrimage itself is 'Hajj'. This means 'to set out with a definite purpose'. The most important thing about a pilgrimage is the spiritual reason for the journey. A pilgrim 'sets out with the definite purpose' of travelling spiritually closer to God. A pilgrimage is a journey made with heart, mind and soul as well as body.

Pilgrimage to Makkah is a duty as

important as prayer or belief in God for Muslims. A Hajji is a very respected person. The drawings on the house in the photograph proudly tell the story of one man's journey to Makkah and the holy places around it. This Hajji lives in a small village in Egypt, where most of the population are Muslims. You'll see paintings and drawings like this on houses in towns and villages all over the country. He is not a rich man. He works hard as a farmer on a small plot of land.

Even though his journey to Makkah was much more comfortable and safe than it would have been 100 years ago, it was still a long and tiring journey. It meant making sacrifices too. The farmer had to save up quite a lot of money. The journey took valuable time when he needed to work in the fields and grow food for his family. He was quite old and frail by the time he had saved enough money to pay for the journey. But he said the day he arrived at Makkah and saw the holy shrine called the Ka'aba was the happiest day of his whole life.

▼ **The paintings on this Egyptian farmhouse show that the owner has made the pilgrimage to Makkah. Can you see pictures of the boat he travelled in to get to Saudia Arabia, the Ka'aba and a mosque with a tall minaret?**

The Hajj

Makkah is in Saudi Arabia. The Muslims who live there and in Egypt are Arabs. Although Arab history and language has played an important part in the religion of Islam, most Muslims are not Arabs. The countries with the largest Muslim populations are Indonesia, Bangladesh, India and Pakistan. There are millions of Muslims in Africa. Islam has more followers in Europe than any religion except Christianity. So the millions of pilgrims who make their way to Makkah each year come from all corners of the earth. Some travel huge distances.

Let's follow the journey of a group of pilgrims from Manchester, England. If you look at the distance between Manchester and Makkah on the map, you'll see they had a long way to travel. What is the longest journey you

▲ Pilgrims live in these tents on the Plain of Arafat, outside Makkah, while they perform the sacred duties of their visit.

have ever made? Perhaps you remember feeling stiff and tired at the end and very pleased to have arrived at last! Years ago it would have taken

the Manchester pilgrims weeks to get to Makkah. But today the journey takes hours rather than days.

Before the journey began, there was a lot of preparation and excitement just as there is before any long journey. But this time there was a special excitement. Most of the Muslims believed that this was the most important journey of their whole lives. Some of them were quite old. A few were ill or weak. Their one wish was to see Makkah and the holy Ka'aba before they died. Before they set off, the pilgrims held a special prayer meeting and asked God's blessing that they might complete their journey.

The pilgrims drove by coach along the motorway to the airport. They showed their tickets and passports and boarded a large aeroplane. It was a long flight but it took them straight to the special Hajj terminal at Jeddah airport. When the pilgrims stepped outside, the fierce heat and dust of Saudi Arabia was a shock. They all felt tired but the thought that they were about to fulfil their dream of a lifetime gave them new energy.

Everyone is equal

One of the first things the pilgrims did was to put on the simple white robes which all pilgrims wear. They make everyone look the same and you can't tell whether a man is rich or poor, a farmer or a businessman. All anyone can tell is that everybody shares the same faith and has travelled to Makkah with the same purpose. This is all that matters. For the pilgrims, wearing the robes is a way of expressing their feeling that everyone is equal in the eyes of God.

Although the pilgrims were of many different nationalities, they didn't need to speak each other's languages to communicate. They understood one another because they shared the same thoughts and the same purpose. They thought only of God and his prophet Muhammad. They were speaking the language of worship.

▼ One of these sacred duties is to throw stones at some stone columns which represent the place where Abraham was tempted by the Devil. All pilgrims wear the same white robes to show that everyone is equal in the eyes of God.

Most pilgrims try to go on the Hajj in the second week of the last month in the Islamic calendar, although pilgrimage may be made at other times too.

After travelling by bus from Jeddah to Makkah, the pilgrims begin a series of acts of worship there and at several sacred places nearby. These take several days and are described on the plan. When the pilgrims from Manchester had completed all the stages of the Hajj, they returned to the airport and flew back to their families and friends. They took with them small bottles of holy water and enough memories of their holy journey to last a lifetime. They were filled with happiness and peace. The ones who had been ill said they felt much better. When they got home they shared their joy and blessings with everyone and proudly called themselves Hajji.

They walk seven times between two hills in Makkah where Ishmael's mother, Hagar, ran searching for water. Ishmael found the spring which turned Makkah into an oasis. Pilgrims collect bottles of this holy water.

Makkah
Pilgrims visit the Ka'aba, the sacred shrine. They walk around it seven times and kiss or touch the black stone set in its wall.

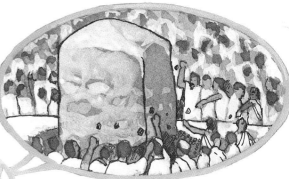

Mina
Here the pilgrims throw stones at three stone pillars. This imitates the way Ishmael drove off the devil who tried to tempt him to do wrong. Then pilgrims sacrifice an animal in memory of Abraham's sacrifice of a ram instead of his son.

Medina
Pilgrims visit the Ka'aba again. Before returning home, they may visit other historic sites, such as the Prophet's Mosque at Medina.

Write about an important journey you once made – perhaps to a foreign country on holiday or to another part of the world to live – or a visit to a special friend or relation. Explain why it was important and how you felt before you set off. Describe the journey and what happened when you arrived.

Arafat
Pilgrims walk or ride the twenty kilometres to the Plain of Arafat and pray there.

Muzdalifah
They return eight kilometres towards Makkah. They say evening prayers and camp in the desert around the village of Muzdalifah.

The Five Pillars of Islam

Making the pilgrimage is one of the five religious duties all Muslims try to keep. These duties are called the Five Pillars of Islam. Pillars is a good word for them because these five duties are the basis on which the Islamic faith is built.

The second of the Five Pillars is that Muslims should pray five times a day, facing the direction of Makkah and the Ka'aba. These prayers can be said alone or with others but everyone is expected to go to the mosque for the noonday prayers on Friday. This is the Muslim holy day.

A Muslim place of worship is called a mosque. A niche hollowed out of one wall in the mosque tells worshippers which is the direction of Makkah. By looking at the map on page 16, can you work out in which direction Makkah lies from England?

Muslims can also use a special compass to find the direction of Makkah. The Manchester pilgrims used one of these when they were travelling by bus and plane to Saudi Arabia. On the way to Manchester airport they were able to stop the coach for a few moments of peaceful prayer. As they did so, they knew they were sharing this act of worship with millions of other Muslims all over the world. All of them would be repeating the same words and gestures, and would have turned towards the same holy place on earth.

The stages of the pilgrimage.

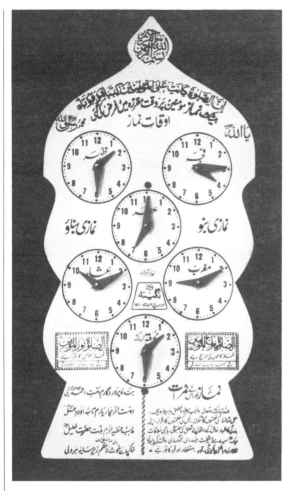

▲ **This board in a London mosque shows the times for the five daily prayers which all Muslims try to perform. The times are based on the rising and setting of the sun so they change during the year.**

dawn and sunrise, between midday and the afternoon, from late afternoon until sunset, after sunset until there's no daylight left, and at night.

If you think about these times for a minute, you'll see how they all come at natural breaks in the day. These are when we get up, around midday (when the sun is fiercest in hot countries and people rest from work for a while), at the end of the working day, after the evening meal and when we go to bed. Which of these natural breaks are you less likely to find in a cool, northern country such as Britain? However, as you can see, each period for prayer lasts several hours. Performing the prayers only takes a few minutes. This means there is usually plenty of time for Muslims, wherever they live and whether they are at home or at work, to find a few quiet minutes for prayer.

Look at the list of times again. Do you see how the timing all depends on the position of the sun? Islam was founded in Arabia, where the sun can usually be seen every day and where

The five daily prayers

Perhaps praying five times a day seems to you quite a hard duty to keep. It shows how important prayer is to Muslims. As we explore the ritual of daily prayer, we'll discover how the ritual actually helps and encourages people to keep this Pillar of Islam.

The prayers should be said between

there is little difference between winter and summer hours of daylight. In northern Europe, however, the hours of prayer in winter will be different from those in summer. Sunset can be as much as five hours earlier in winter than it is in summer.

In Muslim countries a man called a muezzin calls the people to prayer. Usually a mosque has a tall tower, called a minaret, from which the muezzin chants his summons. Even in the Middle East, the sun's position changes a little each day, so the muezzin has an important job to do in letting everyone know the times of prayer. Today, some mosques use loudspeakers so that the muezzin's call can be heard above the noise and bustle of people and traffic. In a northern country such as Britain it is

Imagine you are going to Makkah. Work out your journey using an atlas. Then do a frieze or painting of all the different stages of the journey, showing the distance you will cover and the time it will take. Draw each kind of transport you will use.

often too cloudy to see the sun. There may be a board in the mosque which tells worshippers the times of prayers for that week.

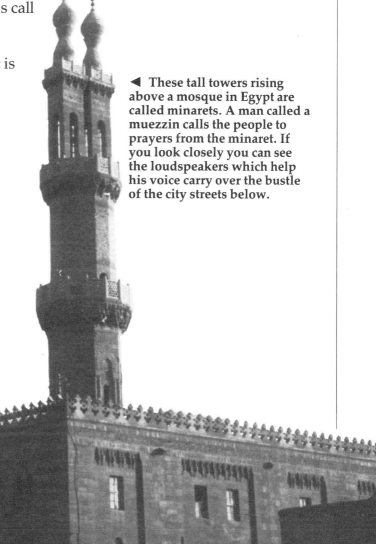

◀ These tall towers rising above a mosque in Egypt are called minarets. A man called a muezzin calls the people to prayers from the minaret. If you look closely you can see the loudspeakers which help his voice carry over the bustle of the city streets below.

◀ Washing before prayer is an important part of the whole act of worship.

The ritual of prayer

Before saying prayers, Muslims wash. This is an important part of the whole act of worship. The worshipper is about to do something very important. He or she is going to talk with God. Pausing to wash gives them time to think about the meaning of what they are going to do. It means they go to their prayers feeling fresh and clean.

It would be difficult to just drop your tools, leave your papers or stop the housework and immediately feel in the right mood for prayer, wouldn't it? Washing means the worshipper feels

in a fit state for prayer and has time to turn his or her mind away from the everyday world to the spiritual one.

Worshippers in a mosque usually follow a prayer leader called an imam. But whether a Muslim is praying alone or with others, they follow the same set of prayer movements you can see here. The sequence of positions and words is called a rakat. A Muslim performs two rakats for morning prayer, four rakats at noon, afternoon and night prayers, and three at sunset. Whatever their nationality, and wherever they live, Muslims pray like this. So worshippers know they are taking part in an act of worship which is the same all over the world and has not changed for over a thousand years.

As you can see, Muslims do not only use words to say their prayers. They use their whole bodies. Movements and gestures can help us to show our feelings about things more clearly. Are there any movements or positions here which you recognise from seeing followers of other religions at prayer? Kneeling or bowing down is a position of worship found in many religions. The word Islam, which is Arabic, actually means 'submission to God'. A Muslim is one who submits to, or obeys, God. The movements and words of the rakat are the language of worship which help Muslims express their feelings of devotion and obedience to God.

The five daily prayers are said to a set of movements. The sequence of words and movements is known as a rakat. A number of rakats are performed each prayer time.

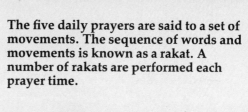

...nds to ears

2
Right hand on
left hand

3
Bowing movement –
hands on knees,
legs straight

4
Return
to upright
position

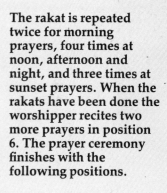

...nk to knees.
...nd forehead to
...ound between
...nds on ground

6
Sit back
on heels,
eyes down.
Hands on
thighs

The rakat is repeated twice for morning prayers, four times at noon, afternoon and night, and three times at sunset prayers. When the rakats have been done the worshipper recites two more prayers in position 6. The prayer ceremony finishes with the following positions.

7
(Kneeling)
Turn head
to look over
right shoulder

8
(Kneeling)
Turn head
to look over
left shoulder

Christian worship

We started this book by thinking about the meaning of worship. We thought about the importance of the idea of 'worth'. We've discovered that for many people religious worship is the way they express their belief that God is worthy of all their respect, honour and love. Then we explored two Muslim acts of worship, which were pilgrimage and prayer. These show us how there can be two parts to worship. There is the outer part, which is usually called the ritual. These are the things people do, which you can see, hear or feel, in order to express their worship. And there is the inner part, which you can't see or touch, which is the belief inside the worshipper. The journey to Makkah and the action of the rakat are the ritual of Muslim pilgrimage and prayer. They are the outer actions which show the inner feelings.

Something else which we learnt in the last chapter is that the ritual of Muslim prayer follows the same pattern, whether the worshipper lives in Manchester or Makkah. One of the things you'll discover in this chapter is that Christian acts of worship are not always performed in exactly the same way. The more you explore Christian worship, the more variety you'll discover. This doesn't mean that the inner part of worship is very different. It just means that Christians have different ways of expressing their faith.

Christian prayer

Prayer has been described as 'a special kind of thinking'. Many people find that using ritual helps them express these special thoughts. It also helps them concentrate on them. For example, the sequence of positions for his body during prayer help a Muslim concentrate his thoughts on God. Praying with eyes closed is common to many religions. It helps people to cut themselves off from the everyday world around them, so that they can concentrate on the spiritual world and be alone with their thoughts of God.

The girl on this page is saying her prayers. Perhaps the position of her body or the way she is holding her hands told you that. Her eyes are shut but she doesn't look sleepy or tired. She looks as though she is thinking.

Make up your own prayer for one of these occasions: the arrival of a baby brother or sister, the start of a new year, the recovery after a bad illness of someone you love.

▶ Prayer has been called a 'special kind of thinking'. Kneeling in this position and closing her eyes helps this girl turn her thoughts away from the things around her and concentrate on the spiritual world.

Do you ever do any 'special kind of thinking'? Perhaps you sometimes feel you want to be alone with your thoughts. You may not feel especially sad or happy. You may simply want to get away from your friends and family to be quiet and by yourself. When you are alone like this, would you say you also felt lonely? There is a difference between being alone and being lonely. When we feel lonely we miss the comfort of other people's company.

The girl on the last page is alone but she doesn't look lonely. She seems rather peaceful and happy. In fact, she looks as though she might be talking and listening to someone in a rather special kind of way. Perhaps that is another way to describe prayer. It is one way in which people can tell God their thoughts and listen to him for comfort and guidance.

People have many different reasons for praying. Sometimes they pray because they want to thank God. This may be for something especially good which has happened but it may just be for being alive! Sometimes people want to say sorry to God for something they have said or done. Sometimes they pray for him to help others, perhaps a friend in trouble or need.

◀ Certain Christians feel that the best way to serve God is to devote their whole lives to prayer. These monks live together in a community called a monastery and have little contact with the world outside.

▼ Some monks and nuns have more contact with people outside their monastery. They may teach or look after the old or the sick.

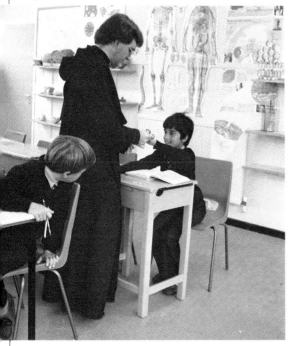

There are many different types of convent or monastery. If there is one near you, try to find out more about it. Perhaps a member of the community could come and talk to your class. If they do, ask them about their daily and weekly timetable. You may find that each member is responsible for different jobs, for example, doing the cooking or organising the music. Find out what these jobs are and decide which one you would like to do.

Then imagine you are a member of the community. Write an account of a typical day in your life.

Sometimes they ask God to help themselves. They may ask him for strength to cope with some sadness or other problem. They may pray for guidance to help them make the right decision about something important.

Prayers may be sung, chanted or said out loud or the worshipper may pray in silence. He or she may kneel to pray, or stand or sit. Worshippers sometimes use a set prayer, such as the Our Father, repeating the same words each time. Sometimes they make up their own words. They may pray together with other people or they may pray alone.

A life of prayer

From the time of the very first Christians, there have always been men and women who have believed that the only way they could truly worship God was by getting away from other people and the everyday world and devoting their whole lives to prayer. These Christians are called monks and nuns. The very first Christians to feel like this were called hermits. They lived completely by themselves, alone with their prayers. But monks live together in monastries and nuns live together in convents.

Some monks and nuns have much more contact with the outside world than others. They may teach in a school or look after the elderly or the sick. Others believe that the best way they can serve God and the world is by prayer alone.

Sharing worship

Like followers of many religions, most Christians like to worship together with others who share their faith. Usually this means taking part in a service which reminds them of their beliefs and gives everyone new strength to follow them in their daily lives. They usually hold the service in a building which is dedicated to religious worship, so that they feel particularly close to God there.

Christian services of worship take many forms but there are two things which are common to them all. Christians offer their worship to God through Jesus Christ, whom they believe is His son. Sunday is the holy day of the week when Christians join together in worship.

We are going to explore the act of worship which is the most important for many Christians. It is called Holy Communion. It is also known as Eucharist, which means 'thanksgiving'. Two other names for it are Mass and the Lord's Supper.

Holy Communion

Holy Communion is a special service which reminds Christians of what happened at the last supper Jesus shared with his disciples. After this meal, Jesus was crucified by his enemies. Yet after his death, he became alive again in a new way to his disciples. He encouraged them to continue his teachings. The disciples went on spreading his message to the world and the Christian Church was born. So Christians believe that Christ's death brought new life and hope to the world.

At the last supper Jesus said "Take, eat, this is my body which is given for you. Do this in remembrance of me". And he broke some bread which everyone shared.

After supper he took a cup of wine and said "Drink this, all of you; for this is my blood of the New Covenant, which is shed for you and for many, for the forgiveness of sins. Do this, as often as you drink it, in remembrance of me."

Ever since, Christians have obeyed his command "Do this, in remembrance of me" by taking part in Holy Communion.

◄ Like followers of many religions, most Christians like to worship together with others who share their religious beliefs. The Christian Church contains different groups of people who do not all worship in exactly the same way. But most of them have a service of worship on Sundays, like these Baptists.

► Christians share bread at Holy Communion, in memory of the last meal Jesus shared with his disciples.

Holy Communion is an important act of worship for many Christians. If you know someone – a vicar, teacher, family friend or relative – who goes to the Communion service often, ask them to explain what happens and why it is important to them. Ask them how they would feel if, for some reason, they couldn't take part in Holy Communion for a year.

◀ At Holy Communion the priest blesses some bread which he then shares with the congregation.

Communion Christians not only remember the events of the Last Supper. They feel closer to Jesus Christ and to each other.

One way of seeing the importance and meaning of this act for Christians is to see them as standing in a long line of people stretching back through history who have performed this same act of worship in all corners of the world. This human chain stretches

During the first part of the Holy Communion service there are readings from the Bible. Then the priest gives a short talk about some part of Christian teaching. Often the congregation then repeat the Creed. The Creed is a statement of their most important beliefs. The priest then blesses some wine and some bread which is shared by the congregation.

As the worshipper receives a piece of the bread, the priest says "the body of Christ" and as they sip the wine he says "the blood of Christ". It is a very vivid and powerful way of obeying Christ's words. Communion means 'coming together'. By taking

▲ The priest shares the bread with his congregation. He blesses them by making the sign of the cross.

◄ The priest makes a sign of the cross over the communion wine to bless it.

back for nearly 2000 years and eventually it reaches Jesus himself. Holy Communion brings Christians in touch with Jesus as a living figure. The service ends with hymns and prayers of thanksgiving, as the congregation join together and thank God for the love he has shown the world through Jesus.

Different ways of worship

Christians believe that in Holy Communion Jesus becomes present among them. Different groups have different beliefs about the way in which this happens. They also use some different forms of ritual in the service.

Some groups sit to receive communion and others stand or kneel. Some share the same cup of wine. Others have small separate glasses of wine. Sometimes only the priest sips the wine. Some churches celebrate Holy Communion on weekdays as well as Sunday. Some do not hold a service every Sunday.

31

Although some of the ritual of Holy Communion may vary from church to church, most Christians feel the same way about its meaning. The service reminds them that Jesus' death was for them and for all the world. He taught them about the love of God and brought them hope and happiness. By taking communion Christians share in the actions of Jesus. They remind themselves that they must also share his unselfishness and his willingness to help others. And by re-living the events of the Lord's Supper in this special and very vivid way, they come closer to God.

Quakers are Christians who believe that all that is necessary to come closer to God is for two or three people to gather together in worship. They meet in a plain room and do not have priests or ministers.

Often there may be silence at their meetings. Sometimes people stand up and share their thoughts with the other worshippers.

Find out how many different groups of Christians worship in your neighbourhood. Are there differences in the way they celebrate Holy Communion?

The Quakers

Although Holy Communion is a very important service to most Christians, some members of the church feel differently about using ritual to express their feelings about God. While some Christians feel they are helped in their worship by buildings full of colour and decoration and services full of ceremony and ritual, others prefer to worship in a plain and simple way. One group like this is the Quakers.

Quakers believe strongly in Jesus' words that "For where two or three come together in my name, I am there with them." (Matthew 18, v 20). They believe that all that is necessary for people to come close to God is for two or three people to gather together in worship. So they have no priests or ministers, no hymns, no communion, nobody wearing special clothes and no building with special furniture such as an altar. Quakers just meet in a plain room, usually on a Sunday morning, and sit on chairs around a table. There may be complete silence for much of the meeting. But it is not a sleepy or thoughtless silence. Like the girl praying (on page 25), the Quakers are thinking in a special way and trying to communicate with God. Somebody might stand up and talk about some experience or idea they have had which they think could help others. But there is no fixed pattern of events at the meetings.

The Quakers are a small group of Christians but they are well known and respected for all the good things they have done to help other people. The purpose of their meeting together is to come closer to God, just as it is for all Christians. The way they worship is different because it is the way which has most meaning for them. It is the language which helps them say most clearly what they feel about God.

The way of the Buddha

Do you remember the picture on the front of this book? It showed a boy who might be about your own age. He is a Buddhist. Buddhists follow the way of life taught by the Buddha, a wise and holy man who lived nearly six hundred years before Jesus was born. His real name was Siddhartha Gautama. The Buddha means 'the one who has become aware of the truth of things'. As you learn about the religion he founded you'll discover why people called him that.

Before you read any further, look carefully at the statue of the Buddha opposite. Think about the sort of feelings the statue seems to show. Does the Buddha look angry or sad? Does he seem irritated or disatisfied or restless in any way? Then ask yourself whether the boy on the cover seems to feel any of these things either. They both seem very calm, don't they? Try to write down three words which describe the mood of the Buddha. Perhaps you would choose one or more of these: calm, peaceful, serene, happy, content, thoughtful or gentle.

Many Buddhists do seem to be rather thoughtful and gentle people. If you aren't a Buddhist and don't know any people who are, perhaps the best way to explore this religion is to start with the story of the Buddha himself. It may help you to understand why some Buddhists do seem to have these special qualities.

The story of the Buddha

Siddhartha Gautama was the son of a rich and powerful man. He lived in what is now the country of Nepal, near the border with India. Soon after he was born, some wise men told his father that Siddhartha would grow up to be a great man. He would either become a warrior and ruler or, they warned, he would leave his family and the palace for good. He would give them up in order to teach ordinary people how to find relief from pain and sorrow and discover true happiness.

His father was sad when he heard this. He decided to protect his son from the discovery that pain or sorrow existed in the world, so that he would never feel he had to leave home. He built three beautiful palaces, for the different seasons of the year. Nobody who was ill or old was allowed near Siddhartha. Some say his father even had fading flowers or dying plants removed from the gardens before Siddhartha could see them, so that he would not know about death.

This statue of the Buddha is in a temple in Burma. Before you turn over the page, stop and look at this picture for a while. What sort of feelings does the Buddha seem to show? Does he seem unhappy or worried? Does he seem to be suffering in some way? Or does he seem peaceful and thoughtful?

Siddhartha's mother dreams of a white elephant. She learns that the meaning of this dream is that she will give birth to a great and noble son.

Siddhartha grows up to be a gentle and thoughtful man. He proved how skilled he was in such war-like arts as archery but he would not fight or hurt others.

Siddhartha marries his beautiful cousin, Yasodhara. They live together in the palaces his father built to protect Siddhartha from ever discovering that suffering and sorrow exist in the world.

One day, Siddhartha leaves the palace grounds. He comes across an old man, a sick man and a dead man – for the first time in his life. He also sees a holy man.

Siddhartha decides he must find a cure for this suffering. He leaves his family, cuts off his hair, and orders his heart-broken servant and horse back to the palace.

Siddhartha searches for the truth about life by studying and meditating. He takes very little food and rest. He grows thin and weak but he finds no answers.

He decides neither a life of luxury nor one of hardship are the right way to live. He starts to follow the Middle Way. After some time he achieves enlightenment and becomes the Buddha. He passes on his teaching to others.

The Buddha dies. His teachings about giving up greed and selfishness and being kind and thoughtful to others are spread all over the world. Today there are about 500 million Buddhists.

The world outside

Siddhartha grew up to be a kind, intelligent and strong man. He married his beautiful cousin and together they lived a life of great luxury. One day, Siddhartha persuaded one of the servants to take him out of the grounds of the palace. What he saw of the world outside the palace walls changed his life.

First Siddhartha saw an old, white-haired man. He was stiff and unsteady on his thin, worn-out legs. Then he came across a man who was ill and in great pain. He rolled on the ground and moaned in agony. Siddhartha didn't know that disease or old age existed. He had never met an ill or an old person in his life. Can you imagine the shock this was to him?

Later he saw a dead man, followed by the weeping family. Siddhartha was horrified. He had never seen such misery and sorrow. Finally, he saw a holy man. He looked so calm and peaceful that it made Siddhartha very thoughtful.

When he returned to the palace he could not forget what he had seen. Why do people die, he wondered? Why was there so much sadness and ugliness in the world? Would all this happen to his own family? It was like a terrible riddle which he couldn't solve. And at the back of his mind was the feeling that the holy man had found some sort of answer to the riddle.

◄ **Some of the episodes from the story of the Buddha's life.**

Think about the episode in the story of the Buddha when the young Siddhartha comes across the old man, the sick man, the dead man and the holy man. Draw your own picture of these meetings.

Looking for answers

Siddhartha decided to leave his family and their lovely home, where no one seemed to die and the flowers never seemed to fade. He had to explore the world outside. He wanted to find a way to end all the suffering he had seen there. He was very sad when he left because he loved his family, but he knew he had a special job to do. Like a doctor who knows he must do everything possible to cure someone, Siddhartha had to find out what was causing people's suffering and find a way to cure it. He had to find the right prescription or medicine.

At first Siddhartha tried living a hard, uncomfortable life. He changed his fine clothes for rags. He ate little and slept outside on the hard ground. After six years he looked a bit like a skeleton. But he was no nearer to finding the answers to his questions. He realised that neither his old life of luxury nor this harsh existence were the right ways to live. He began to believe that a middle way, in between both those kinds of life, was the best.

37

Nirvana

Siddhartha began to eat properly and soon felt stronger. He concentrated even harder on finding the answers to the questions in his mind. He sat by himself under the shade of a large Bo tree, alone with his thoughts. After many weeks of deep concentration he felt he had finally learnt the truth about life. He managed to clear his mind of everything which had distracted and confused him. He achieved what Buddhists called 'Nirvana'. He became the Buddha, one who is aware of the truth about things.

▼ Lobsang is a young Buddhist in Nepal training to be a monk. Here he is in the classroom at the monastery near Kathmandu where he lives.

The Middle Way

Do you remember the feelings of peace and contentment there seemed to be about the Buddha on page 35? Then you may be a little surprised to discover that one of the first things which the Buddha realised was that pain and suffering *are* part of our lives. We can't escape them. But listen to what else he said.

Much of this suffering is caused by the fact that nothing in life ever stays the same, not even ourselves. We all change as we grow up. Everyone has to grow old and die. We feel sad and disappointed when we don't get what we want or when we have to leave behind people, situations or things that we like. But if we could stop feeling angry about this and accept it as part of life, it wouldn't make us so unhappy. The Buddha said that our unhappiness comes from our greed and selfishness. We are always wanting the wrong things, or the right things in the wrong way. And the more we want, the less happy we are. If we could stop wanting things so much, then we would not constantly suffer the disappointment of not getting exactly what we want.

So the Buddha worked out a way of life which would help people to stop wanting the very things which in the end make them unhappy. He called it the Middle Way. Do you remember where that phrase was used before? It was when the Buddha had decided to follow a lifestyle in between total luxury and total hardship. So do you think following the Middle Way is likely to mean giving up everything in life we enjoy? From what we have already learnt, it is more likely to mean finding a thoughtful and balanced way to live and giving up greed and selfishness.

▶ An older monk shows Lobsang some Buddhist scriptures. Lobsang is learning maths, English, Tibetan reading and writing, and the history and teachings of his religion.

The Eight-fold Path

Buddhists believe that by following this Middle Way, they will get closer to finding the same peace and understanding that the Buddha finally achieved. In order to do this they must follow the Eight-fold Path. These are eight guidelines for living which are the Buddha's prescription to cure suffering. The eight guidelines describe ways of thinking, feeling and behaving which help people free themselves from the suffering and sorrow caused by greed and selfishness.

One or two of them may be a little difficult to understand at first. Right mindfulness and right concentration mean being aware all the time of what you are doing. This means never being thoughtless or careless and so hurting others by your actions. It means not giving into selfish thoughts. It means doing things well and concentrating on them and on nothing else, however small that task may be. Try doing that next time you help out in the garden or with the housework. It is not as easy as it sounds.

When the Buddha died he was 80 years old. His teaching had spread all over the area which is now north and eastern India. Today, there are more

Think of eight different ways of thinking, doing things, feeling and behaving to people which you think would help you and others to lead a happier life. Write them down and then compare your list with the Buddha's Eight-fold Path.

2 Right values to understand the real worth of things. Being selfish is a wrong value. Being kind is a right value.

1 Right viewpoint to look at life from the right point of view.

8 Right concentration to learn how to control your mind so that you can concentrate completely on your search for truth and knowledge.

7 Right mindfulness to carefully consider everything you do and not give into selfish thoughts.

THE EIGHT-FOLD PATH
The Buddha's eight guidelines for living are shown here, arranged around the wheel of life. This is an important Buddhist symbol. It stands for the cycle of birth, life, death and re-birth.

3 Right speech
not to lie
or boast but to
be kind and
helpful in
what you say.

4 Right behaviour
to behave well
and not to,
for example,
steal.

5 Right living
to follow a
way of earning
a living which
doesn't harm
others.

6 Right effort
to avoid evil
thoughts and
actions and work
at developing
good ones.

than five hundred million Buddhists in the world. Most Buddhists live in Asia but more and more people in Europe and North America are finding the Buddha's teaching helps them make sense of their lives.

A young Buddhist

Lobsang is a Buddhist. That's him on page 38, sitting in the classroom of the monastery in Nepal where he lives. Lobsang is training to be a monk. He is only ten years old. He came to the monastery when he was seven. His family live nearby in Kathmandu, the capital of Nepal. Lobsang often goes home to see them. Some boys' parents live a long way away and they only visit them once or twice a year. Lobsang did miss his family at first but now he loves his life in the monastery.

He says he has lots of friends and that the older monks are kind and always ready to explain things he doesn't understand. Lobsang is learning maths, English, Tibetan reading and writing, and religion. He finds maths rather difficult but he loves listening to the Buddhist scriptures. These contain the Buddha's teachings and many stories about his life. The scriptures are written in Tibetan. Lobsang is too young to read and understand them all. He knows it will take many years before he is as wise as the older monks.

▲ Lobsang reads some prayers. They teach him to be kind and thoughtful in everything he does and to give up any greedy or selfish ideas.

◄ Lobsang with some of his friends who are also learning to follow the Buddhist way of life. Some may decide to leave the monastery when they are about fifteen. Others will stay on to become monks. In Buddhist countries young boys often spend some time in a monastery, although it may only be a few months.

Every morning the monks gather in the temple to chant their prayers. Lobsang still has to read most of them but he is beginning to learn quite a few by heart. When he is about fifteen Lobsang may decide to leave the monastery. He might start work in his father's shop in Kathmandu. At the moment he thinks he would rather stay in the monastery.

In the temple where Lobsang says his prayers there is a huge statue of the Buddha, rather like the one on page 35. In front of the statue the monks lay offerings – grains of rice, flowers, bowls of water, incense and candles. It is quite dark in the temple but not gloomy. Two large lamps burn all day and night. At prayertime lots of tiny oil lamps and candles flicker and glow.

Setting an example

Buddhists believe the Buddha was a wise and holy man who set an example to them. They do not think of him as a god. He showed a way to live which could bring peace and understanding to those who follow it. But the offerings made by Buddhists to the Buddha in their homes and temples are very like some of the other acts of worship we have explored. They remind the offerer of the reasons why they must follow the way that the Buddha showed them. They remind Buddhists that it is only by their own efforts to follow the Middle Way that they will achieve the peace and understanding that the Buddha showed them was possible.

So when Lobsang places some offerings in front of the temple statue, his act of worship is a way of showing what Buddha's teachings mean to him. The candle he lights reminds him of the light of understanding he hopes to achieve by following the Eight-fold Path. Enlightenment is another word to describe the Nirvana the Buddha achieved. The flowers Lobsang offers soon wilt and fade. They remind him that everything in life must change and that it is foolish to try to cling on to things in life as if they belonged to us. We must recognise that nothing stays the same. Only the truth is everlasting and unchanging.

Meditation

When we started to explore the idea of prayer on page 24, we thought about it being a 'special kind of thinking'. We thought about the times when we want to be by ourselves and think quietly. One important way in which many Buddhists try to find greater peace and understanding of life is by a kind of deep thought called meditation. Lobsang is only just beginning to learn to meditate but if he described it to you he might also call it a 'special kind of thinking'. It means concentrating very hard on one idea and clearing your head of all the other untidy thoughts which keep straying in.

This is what the Buddha did when he sat quietly by himself under the Bo tree and achieved Nirvana. He cleared his mind of everything that might distract him from finding the truth about life. Lobsang is learning to follow his example. His prayers and meditation help him to concentrate on the Buddha's wise teachings and follow the Middle Way.

When we first started to explore what people mean by worship, right at the beginning of this book, one of the feelings we thought about was admiration. We also thought about wanting to follow a way of life or somebody's example, because they seem to be able to do and understand things which we find difficult or puzzling. We explored some of the

◄ Like the girl on page 25, this young Buddhist is concentrating on a 'special kind of thinking'. It is called meditation. It helps him to understand the wise teachings of the Buddha and to learn to follow the Middle Way in his own life.

Look through the adverts in some colour supplements and magazines. Make a list of eight things which you and your family would really like to have. Cut out pictures of them and stick these up together.

Then think back to your birthday a year ago and remember the presents you wanted then. Do you still use them and play with them? Do they still make you happy, and mean as much to you now as they did?

Now look back at the eight pictures of the things you and your family want at the moment. Why do you think they will make you happy? Do you think they will mean as much to you in a year's time?

Write down what you feel about the way people always seem to want things to make them happy. How does it fit in with what you have learnt about the teachings of the Buddha?

things about life which people find hard to accept and have always questioned. We discovered that religious belief has helped many people find some of the answers to these questions.

How do these ideas and thoughts fit in with what you now know about Buddhism? Perhaps you can see how Buddhism has helped some people answer their questions about life, just as Islam and Christianity have helped others. Maybe the story of the Buddha and his teachings has also helped you to understand why there is such a calm and peaceful feeling about his statue and why Lobsang wants to follow his example.

45

There have been a number of activities in this book which have asked you to write about something, draw a picture or find things out. You might like to put all these in one book and call it *My Own Book of Worship*.

Here are some suggestions for more work which could go into your *Book of Worship*.

Write about other centres of pilgrimage, such as Jerusalem, Canterbury, Rome or Lourdes, and what they mean to the pilgrims who travel there.

Explore the different ways people use music in religious worship.

Find out how people use holy writings in worship – both when they worship alone and with others.

Look at these pictures of Buddhist prayer flags waving in the wind. People put them there in the hope that the good thoughts of the prayers and the wise words of the scriptures written on the flags will be carried away on the wind far and wide.

How would you describe a prayer? Make up some prayers for peace and understanding which you would like to write on a prayer flag so that they might spread out to the whole world.

Glossary and Index

altar 33   a table-like object in a church at which Holy Communion is celebrated

Bible 30   the holy book of Christianity, made up of the Old Testament (the complete Jewish Bible) and the New Testament

Christian Church the world-wide community of Christians

Eight-fold Path 40, 43   the Buddha's eight guidelines for living

enlightenment 36, 38, 43, 45   seeing 'the light' and understanding the truth about life; the state of mind the Buddha achieved, called Nirvana by Buddhists

Five Pillars of Islam 19   five duties which all Muslims try to keep; they are described in the holy book of Islam, the Qur'an

Hajj 15   pilgrimage to Makkah undertaken by Muslims; one of the Five Pillars of Islam

Hajji, Hajjin 15, 18   title given to men and women respectively who have completed the Hajj

Holy Communion 28–31   service in which Christians remember Jesus' last meal with the disciples; also called Eucharist, the Last Supper or Mass

imam 22   Muslim prayer leader and teacher of religion.

Ka'aba, the 14–17, 19   holy shrine in Makkah; Muslims all over the world turn in its direction to pray

Makkah (Mecca) 12, 14–19   the holiest city in the religion of Islam; it is in Saudi Arabia

meditation 36, 45   a kind of deep thought

Middle Way, the 36–40, 43   the Buddha's teaching that people should live a life of neither total luxury nor great discomfort

minaret 21   tall tower of a mosque from which the muezzin calls Muslims to prayer

monks 27, 41, 43   men who have devoted their lives to prayer and worship; they usually live and work together in monasteries

mosque 19, 21, 22   Muslim building of worship and religious education

muezzin 21   person who calls Muslims to prayer

Muhammad 17   the prophet of Islam, to whom God revealed the words of the Qur'an

Muslims   followers of the religion of Islam

Nirvana,   *see* enlightenment

nuns 27   women who have devoted their lives to prayer and worship; they usually live and work together in convents

pilgrimage 12, 15–18   journey to sacred place, or person, undertaken as an act of worship

prayer 24–26, 45
  Christian 24
  Muslim 19–23

priest   person who can carry out religious ceremonies

Quakers 32–33   a group of Christians who worship God in simple gatherings without ceremony or ritual

rakat 22–23   the sequence of words and actions which are performed a set number of times by Muslims at their five daily prayers

ritual 12, 22, 24, 31, 33   the outer movements and words which help people express their inner religious beliefs

sacred   something which has religious meaning or importance

scriptures 39, 41, 46   the sacred writings of any religion

soul 9   the part of people which is thought of as separate from the body; followers of most religions believe the soul or spirit lives on after the body dies

Tibetan 41   the language of the Tibetan people, who are Buddhists

Wheel of Life 40–41   Buddhist symbol which stands for the cycle of life, death and re-birth

Acknowledgements

The author would like to thank David Naylor for his unfailing enthusiasm for the series and invaluable advice. Thanks are also due to the Regional Religious Education Centre of the West London Institute of Education, the Mid-Hampshire Teachers' Centre, R Hodson, Alan Brine, Elaine Bellchambers, Mr Syed and particularly all those who read and commented on the manuscripts. A special thanks to the Rev Bill Ind, Rabbi David Freeman, Imam Abdul Rahman and all those they work with, for their help and patience in talking about their daily lives.

The publishers would like to thank the following for permission to reproduce photographs and illustrations.

AMENA 14
Olivia Bennett 20/21, 38, 39, 42, 43, 46
Camera Press 13(B), 16, 17
Christopher Cormack/Impact Photos 13(T), 26, 27
Daily Telegraph Colour Library 6/7
Richard and Sally Greenhill 28
Mrs S Owen 36
Ann and Bury Peerless Slide Resources and Picture Library 35
The Library Committee of the Religious Society of Friends 33
David Richardson 25, 29, 32
Liba Taylor 15, 20, 22, 23, 30, 31, 44

Cover picture: a novice monk, Burma (Camerapix Hutchison Library)

Picture research by Caroline Paines and Olivia Bennett.